A Codex on Creating a Magical Phantom

Magic Quest, Volume 1

Gideon Crusader

Published by Gideon Crusader, 2022.

While every precaution has been taken in the preparation of this book, the publisher assumes no responsibility for errors or omissions, or for damages resulting from the use of the information contained herein.

A CODEX ON CREATING A MAGICAL PHANTOM

First edition. November 6, 2022.

Copyright © 2022 Gideon Crusader.

ISBN: 979-8215317471

Written by Gideon Crusader.

Also by Gideon Crusader

Magic Quest
A Codex on Creating a Magical Phantom

Table of Contents

For Kit & Frater K.Y.S.

Introduction

Magic Quest: A Codex on Creating a Magical Phantom is a direct and easy to understand manual that teaches the art of creating the so-called magical phantom. What is a magical phantom? It is a creation of the magus, and it serves him in whatever purpose he desires. This magical craft has existed for centuries. A thorough research on the history of magic will reveal that this ancient art has been practiced by witches and wizards for centuries. To this day, true practitioners of magic employ magical phantoms to make their will manifest on all planes of existence, as well as to have a strong and trustworthy magical ally.

Magic Quest: A Codex on Creating a Magical Phantom reveals the essential teachings and knowledge that you need to start creating your very own magical phantom. By the time you finish reading this codex, you will have unlocked the secrets behind this magical mystery.

Magic Quest: A Codex on Creating a Magical Phantom will not only teach you how to create the legendary magical phantom, but it will also develop your overall magical faculties. If you are willing to put in the time and effort to learn this magical technique, then you will be able to cast real and powerful magic. Indeed, this kind of magic is learnable as long as you know the right instructions. After gaining the right knowledge, it is up to you to put the teachings into actual and continuous practice toward mastery of the technique.

Are you ready to embark on a journey of real magic? If yes, then let me know welcome you into this magical universe where you shall awaken the power that lies within and where your desires shall be the very laws that govern the universe. Welcome into this world of eternal magic.

What is a Magical Phantom?

A magical phantom is a magical creature that is created by a magician or witch. It is a really helpful magical ally to have on your journey because it will serve you to the best of its abilities. It should be noted that a magical phantom usually has very little intelligence, and this is actually a good thing because it will simply do whatever you command it without any discrimination or preference. As you can see, once you have a magical ally such as this, a whole world of possibilities shall open right before you.

A magical phantom is also known by other names, such as a magical elementary, servitor, guardian, or even a witch's astral familiar, among others. It should be noted, however, that a magical phantom exists in the astral plane. What is the astral plane? It is the dimension where spirits belong, as well as thoughts and the imagination come alive. The magical phantom does not have a physical existence, but it can affect the physical plane.

Various occult researches have been conducted proving that a disease first manifests in the astral plane before it can have any manifestation in the physical place. This means that the physical plane is created and is made manifested from the astral dimension. It then follows that whatever you do in the astral dimension can have its manifestation in the physical dimension.

A magical phantom is your magical helper. It will do whatever you command it to do. However, this does not mean that you should abuse your powers. Remember the universal rule that whatever you do shall come back to you. It is strongly suggested that you only use this magic for doing good and good alone. You shall be solely responsible for the consequences of your magic.

Creating a magical phantom is not difficult. It is even possible to successfully create one even on your very first attempt. There are also various ways to create a magical phantom. As long as the governing magical principles are applied, a magical phantom can be created. We will discuss the actual steps later in this book. For now, it is important that you have the right foundational understanding of what a magical phantom really is.

You can think of your magical phantom as some kind of a magical pet. Just like a regular pet, you should also take good care of it. It is also not unusual for magical practitioners to develop some form of bond or even love for their magical phantom. However, it should be noted that you must keep your emotions in check. You should always be in control of your magical phantom, not the other way around. After all, your magical phantom is your servant. You must not allow it to influence or control you in any way.

Let us now talk about the lifespan of a magical phantom. The life of your magical phantom may be as short or as long as you want it to be. It can be as short as a few hours or even a few minutes, but it can also be as long as months or even years. I know some witches who program their magical phantom in such a way that it would be alive for as long as the witch is alive. However, if you are just starting out, it is good to limit the life of your magical phantom for only about three days up to a week. In the beginning, especially if you are still learning the art of creating a magical phantom, you must first familiarize yourself with the actual steps and practice of magical phantom creation. Once you gain more experience and confidence, then you can naturally and easily increase the lifespan of your magical phantom as you develop even more skills and gain more experience.

Just like everything else in the universe, a magical phantom is made of magical energy, which now leads us to our next topic: magical energy.

On Magical Energy

Everything in the universe is made of magical energy. A magical phantom is also made of magical energy. But, what exactly is magical energy? Magical energy or simply *energy* is the force that governs all forms of magic. All spells and rituals depend on how effectively one can harness and manipulate the energy of the universe.

Magical energy is abundant and it is everywhere. It is inside you and all around you. In fact, whenever you feel that you are a stranger to this energy, just remember this magical wisdom: you are made of magical energy. As you can see, you are very much connected to this energy all the time for you are this energy, just as everything around you is also made of this same energy. Therefore, never think or feel that you are a stranger to this energy. Feeling separated from this energy will only make it difficult for you to control and manipulate it.

Let us now discuss certain qualities of magical energy that you must know as a magical practitioner. This magical energy is infinite, and it is everywhere. It is all inside you and outside of you. All things, visible and invisible, are made of this same magical force. Magical energy cannot be killed or destroyed, but it is merely transmuted from one form into another. Interestingly, even conventional science has confirmed that energy cannot die but is only transmuted from state to state, from one form into another.

In its unharnessed state, magical energy is very much neutral and merely follows the regular flow of nature. However, in the hands of a skillful magician or witch, this same magical force can do wonders. But how do you tap and harness this magical energy? The key lies in the use of the mind, especially with the use of the magical imagination.

According to an ancient saying, all things are of the mind. It follows that by gaining mastery and control over one's mind, you can also gain mastery and control over all things in the universe. You must not forget that as a magical practitioner, your mind is your most powerful weapon.

Here is a magical teaching that you must know: energy follows thought. Therefore, as a magical practitioner, you must be very careful with the thoughts that you keep and entertain in your mind. Thoughts are things; and if you are not careful, your mind may be filled with so much negativity and garbage, thereby preventing you from working and creating any significant magic.

From now on, take responsibility over your mind. Your mind is also your sacred and private magical place. It should be noted that in this modern world, it is very easy to be misdirected and have our mind bombarded with so many thoughts and things. Unfortunately, most of these thoughts, if not all, have a negative nature. If you do not take active effort in cleansing and organizing your thoughts, you will easily fall prey to the negative system and way of thinking of this world, and such a mindset is not suitable for a true magical practitioner.

But how does one control and still the mind? Is this even possible? The answer to this is a resounding yes, and the key lies in the practice of meditation.

Meditation

Meditation is a way to still the mind, as well as to free it from the garbage that the world continuously throws at you. If you have noticed, especially in this modern world, so many people are bombarded with countless thoughts. Unfortunately, most of these thoughts are negative. In the long run, if you do not do anything about this, it will definitely have bad effects on you, even on your physical health. Now, the practice of meditation allows us to free ourselves from the many illusions of the modern world. It calls us back to our original source and keeps us calm and peaceful.

Many people are intimidated when they encounter the word *meditation*. You must understand that meditation is actually very easy and simple. In fact, it is more about not doing anything rather than having to do something. Indeed, everyone can meditate, including you. Therefore, do not ever think that meditation is difficult because it is not. A monk even had a joke that anyone who can fall asleep also has the ability to meditate. His point, of course, is that literally everyone can meditate.

In the practice of the magical arts, the practice of meditation is also very important. Meditation unclogs the mind and allows us to achieve the so-called *magical mindset*. The magical mindset is the state of mind that is suitable for the practice of magic.

In this modern time, many people have the wrong understanding that meditation is simply a way to destress and relax. Although distressing and relaxing are a part of the many benefits of meditation, it should be noted that meditation means so much more. Meditation is, first and foremost, a spiritual practice. Through continuous practice, meditation can elevate the soul of man to the Divine.

As you can see, there are so many benefits that you can enjoy when you practice meditation. In the beginning, it may take some discipline for you to actually spend time and effort to meditate; however, once you have adjusted to it, you will realize that meditation is actually a time for spiritual leisure and relaxation. It is no longer a kind of obligation or work that you have to do, but it is actually something that you would gladly do for yourself and for the good of your soul.

The best and only way to understand what meditation really is is through actual and personal experience. The meditation technique that you are now about to learn has been in existence for many centuries. It uses a power word known as a *mantra*. A mantra is a point of focus in meditation. For this meditation, you are going to use the mantra *AUM* (also known as and can be pronounced as *OM*). This mantra is also believed to be the very first sound in the universe. Having said that, here are the steps:

Assume a comfortable position and relax. You can meditate in any comfortable position. However, It is well to note that the sitting position is believed to be the most ideal position for meditation. Even the great Buddha achieved enlightenment while sitting under a tree.

Close your eyes and empty your mind. If thoughts arise in the mind, which they usually do, simply ignore them. Do not use any kind of force. Meditation is a moment of total relaxation and calmness, and it is never about the use of force.

Begin to chant your mantra: AUM/OM. Say it gently and repeatedly. As you are saying your mantra, gently focus on it. You should focus on your mantra in exclusion of all other thoughts and things. Nothing must exist in the mind but the mantra.

In the beginning, you may have to say your mantra out loud or in a form of a whisper; but later on, you will be able to stop saying the mantra physically and yet still be able to hear it internally. This is something that will naturally come about through continuous practice.

Simply focus gently on your mantra and be one with it. Nothing must exist in the mind but your mantra. Your mantra is your spiritual vehicle that will lead you to a higher level of consciousness and being. AwwContinue this meditation for as long as comfortable and for as long as you want.

You may end this meditation by gently bringing your awareness and attention back to your physical body. Once you can sense your body again, slowly move your fingers and those, and very gently open your eyes.

The meditation technique that we have just discussed is a simple yet very powerful meditation practice. In fact, the practice of this meditation alone would be enough to significantly develop your magical and spiritual faculties.

Another meditation technique that you should learn is what is known as meditation on the breath. This meditation technique is probably the simplest form of meditation, and yet it is also very powerful. It is very similar to the meditation technique that we have just discussed; however, instead of focusing on a mantra, you will be focusing on your breath. Here are the steps:

Take a comfortable position and relax. Close your eyes and clear your mind. Just relax and be still. Breathe through your nose. Now, gently focus on your breathing. If thoughts arise in the mind, ignore them by bringing your attention always back to your breath. Breath is life. Therefore, he who meditates on the breath, actually meditates on life. There are so many people who take their breaths for granted, failing to realize that a sudden and simple break in this breathing cycle would mean the total demise of their physical body. As a magical practitioner, we must not take anything for granted; but instead, we must know the importance of everything, including the little things.

Continue to focus on your breath in exclusion of any and all other thoughts. Continue for as long as you like. At any time that you want to end this meditation, simply bring yourself back to your body, gently move your fingers and toes, and slowly open your eyes.

If you are serious about achieving any significant and serious progress in your magical journey, then the practice of meditation should be prioritized. I know many people who want to develop their spirituality and magical abilities but fail to do so simply because they do not make time to meditate. You must realize that nobody will prioritize your magical and spiritual practices but only yourself. Considering the modern world, it is very easy to be manipulated and misdirected. Therefore, a true magical practitioner must exert effort and make time for their magical and spiritual duties.

There are no heart and fast rules on how many times one should meditate. However, the general suggestion is that one should meditate at least twice daily. Take note that this is only the minimum suggested requirement. Of course, if you can do so much more, then it would be more beneficial for you. From now on, make the practice of meditation a natural part of your daily life. If you do this, you will definitely see significant and positive changes soon.

The practice of meditation is very important if you want to learn the art of creating and using a magical phantom. Meditation will naturally allow you to achieve the magical mindset, which is the mindset that is optimum for magical work. It should also be noted that even if you follow all the steps and all the procedures by the very letter, if you do not have the right state of mind, then you cannot expect to have any positive result. Never forget that all things are of the mind, even magic is mental. Therefore, you must work on the very source of your magic, which is your mind. Develop your mind and your magic will also grow.

Basic Magical Phantom (Quick & Easy Method)

Let us now talk about the actual creation of a magical phantom. The technique that you are about to learn is the quick and easy method to create a magical phantom. Nevertheless, if you do it correctly and if you practice enough, this technique will allow you to create a powerful magical phantom. Before we discuss the actual steps, remember that breath is life. Energy is also in the breath. By learning to use the breath in a magical way, it can be a powerful source of power.

The technique that you are about to learn harnesses the power of the breath and uses it to create a magical phantom. Never forget that a magical phantom is your servant. You are the god of your magical phantom. Having said that, here are the steps:

Assume a comfortable position and relax. You may meditate for a few minutes if you want, but it is not necessary. Now, once your mind is clear and still, imagine your magical phantom right in front of you. It can be in any form or image that you want. If you are just starting out, it is good to visualize your magical phantom simply as a ball of white light. Imagine your magical phantom as vividly as you can.

The next step is to breathe life into your magical phantom. This will finally put it into existence as a living being. To do this, blow into your magical phantom six times. According to sacred scriptures, God created the world in 6 days. Hence, you will blow six breaths into your magical phantom for its creation and manifestation. As you blow into your magical phantom, know in your mind that you are breathing life into it. Having this intention alone will activate the power of the breath to give life to your magical phantom. After the sixth breath, know that your magical phantom is now in existence.

The next step is to give your magical phantom a name. Everything in existence in the universe has a name; by giving your magical phantom a name, you further emphasize and establish its existence and reality. When it comes to naming your magical phantom, you are free to choose whatever name you want it to be called. However, it is suggested that you must give it a name that other people will not be able to guess easily. The reason for this is that names have power. A dark wizard may be able to call and even manipulate your magical phantom by its name. But, if they fail to identify the name of your magical phantom, it would be very difficult for them to connect and especially manipulate your magical phantom. Therefore, choose a name that would be impossible to guess and make sure to keep this name a secret.

Naming your magical phantom is easy. You just have to tell it, "Your name is _______________" Say this three times to emphasize to your magical phantom the name by which it is now called.

After giving a name to your magical phantom, you can now communicate to your magical phantom its purpose or function. There are two ways of doing this: verbally and by the use of the imagination. To do it verbally, you just have to give your command to your magical phantom but be careful to observe the basic rules on making an affirmation. The rules are as follows:

- Keep it short and simple

- Use the present tense

- Believe in whatever you are saying

- Use the power of repetition

For example, if you want to command your magical phantom to protect you from all psychic attacks, simply tell your magical phantom, "Protect me from all psychic attacks." Say this at least thrice to give more emphasis.

The next and final step is the sending out of your magical phantom. This is the part where you finally send the magical phantom out into the universe for it to do its purpose.

This is very easy to do. Simply do a gesture to signify and communicate that you are now sending it out for it to finally do its function. This can be as simple as a wave of a hand or a wand, a snap of a finger, or even a verbal command saying, "Go and do it now." As you do this, imagine your magical phantom moving and now doing its specified task.

If you have reached this part and have done so successfully in your own practice, then congratulations. As you can see, creating a magical phantom is easy to do as long as you know how to do it properly. Creating a magical phantom is one thing, taking good care of it is another. If you want to keep your magical phantom for a long period, you should take care of it as you would any other pet or familiar, and this leads us to our next topic.

Taking Care of Your Magical Phantom

If you want to keep your magical phantom with you, then you should take good care of it. The good news is that you do not need to spend any money to take perfect care of your magical phantom. Keep in mind that your magical phantom has its existence in the astral plane, not in the physical plane. Still, even though your magical phantom is in the astral plane, it can affect and influence the physical plane directly.

So how exactly do you take care of your magical phantom? Remember that all things in the universe are made of magical energy. This magical energy is inside you and all around you. If you want to take care of your magical phantom, then you must feed it with magical energy. It should be noted that a magical phantom has very little intelligence. On its own, it does not know how to take care of itself. If you do not feed it with magical energy, it will soon starve itself to death and simply disappear. To prevent this from happening, you should be responsible enough to look after your magical phantom and feed it with magical energy. Do not worry, this is easy to do. Simply imagine your magical phantom right in front of you or call it by its name. Visualize your magical phantom as clearly as you can. Now, imagine magical energy all around you. You may visualize the magical energy in any way that you want. If you are just starting out, it is highly recommended to imagine magical energy as being made of pure white light. In fact, I know many advanced practitioners who still like to imagine magical energy as being made of nothing else but pure white light. The important thing is to know in your mind that what you are visualizing is magical energy.

The next step is to harness this magical energy and feed it into your magical phantom. To do this, see and feel that you are drawing the magical energy and pressing it into your magical phantom, which in turn, receives it gladly. Imagine your magical phantom as some kind of sponge that greedily absorbs the magical energy, thereby empowering itself.

Continue to feed magical energy to your magical phantom. Once you feel that your magical phantom is fully recharged with energy, you may stop visualizing the magical energy. Look at your magical phantom and see and feel that it is powerful once again. Remember that you should feed your magical phantom with energy every now and then. Do not worry, once your magical phantom gains more ability and experience, it will be able to become self-sufficient. It will soon have the ability to survive on its own. This means that it will be able to feed itself with magical energy without your help. On average, it usually takes about a month before a phantom learns this ability of survival. Take note, however, that you must take good care of your phantom, and be sure that it will not wreak havoc. You must keep your magical phantom under your control at all times. It is very risky to allow your magical phantom to have so much power that it can decide on its own without your permission and consent. In history, there have been tragedies where a magical phantom became so powerful that it attacked even its creator, the magician or witch themselves.

A magical phantom begins with very little intelligence and ability. However, as time goes by and it continues to exist, it can become stronger and learn new abilities and skills. This is actually good if you have your magical phantom well within your control; however, if you do not have absolute control over your phantom, this can be a serious problem. Therefore, always remember that you must make it very clear to your magical phantom that you are its master and its god. You must also not show any weakness to your magical phantom. Your magical phantom must know that you can obliterate it at any time you want without any hesitation. It is not good to give your magical phantom any feeling of comfort that it can disobey you or that you will lightly forgive it for any failure to obey you. The key to control is fear. Fear is also what is commonly and effectively used on humans to make us comply and be easily manipulated. The same power of fear applies when it comes to exercising control over your magical phantom.

When you are in contact with your magical phantom just as when you call its name to appear right before you, be sure to always appear strong and powerful. Never show any weakness to your magical phantom as this may have adverse consequences. It is also not uncommon for magical phantoms to confuse kindness for weakness. Therefore, even though you may be tempted to treat your magical phantom as a deer and beloved pet, be sure to keep your emotions in check. You cannot be too close and too caring for your phantom. You must always appear strong and powerful when you are dealing with it. This way, you can ensure that your magical phantom will always fear you; and therefore, be always subject to your will.

It is good to feed your magical phantom with magical energy at least once daily. This will ensure that your magical phantom will have enough energy to survive and to perform whatever task you have given to it.

Basically speaking, to take care of your magical phantom means nothing more than just feeding it with energy. And, at the same time, always make sure to keep the proper kind of relationship that you have with it. You can still be kind to your magical phantom, but not too kind so as to be abused. Remember to always be in control and exercise absolute dominion over your magical phantom. This may sound quite harsh, but this will save you from any adverse consequences that may happen if ever a magical phantom gets out of control and becomes an enemy. Therefore, it is important to exercise all the necessary precautions as early as possible.

The creation of a magical phantom that we have previously discussed may seem simple and easy, but never underestimate its effectiveness and power. With regular practice, the said method will just be as effective as any other methods of creating a magical phantom. Having said that, let us now discuss the standard way of creating a magical phantom.

Standard Magical Phantom Creation

Let us now discuss the standard method of creating a magical phantom. You are free to make adjustments to this method as you may deem necessary in accordance with your own personal preferences, but without sacrificing the very spirit of these teachings. The following method may take a longer step than the one that we have already discussed, but this method is also more effective, and it also has a higher success rate of creating a powerful and genuine magical phantom. Having said that, the steps are as follows:

Assuma comfortable position and relax. You may close your eyes if you want. Now, imagine your magical phantom right in front of you. Again, you can make your magical phantom look any way you want. If you are just starting out, it is suggested to visualize your magical phantom as a ball of white light floating right in front of you. Imagine your magical phantom as vividly as you can.

The next step is to charge your magical phantom with magical energy right away. To do this, imagine magical energy all around you. Again, you may visualize this magical energy in any way that you want. Now, see and feel that you are drawing this magical energy and pouring that energy into your magical phantom, thereby empowering it. Continue feeding your magical phantom with energy to make it stronger and stronger. If you do this correctly, you should be able to see your magical phantom shining brightly with your mind's eye. This is a natural psychic response to what you are doing in the astral plane.

The next step is similar to the previous method that we have discussed. Blow six times into your magical phantom, thereby charging it with your own breath and thus giving life to it. Know that your magical phantom is in existence, it is time to give it a name. Simply follow the procedure as we have previously discussed in giving a name to your magical phantom, which is as simple as saying, "Your name is ___________."

The next step is to give your command to your magical phantom. Again, follow the procedure as we have already previously discussed. This is the part where you give to your magical phantom its very purpose for existing. Be sure to use both the verbal method and imaginative method to effectively and powerfully communicate and impress upon your magical phantom its purpose.

The next step, which is not a part of the process in the other method that we discussed, is giving a particular timeline to your magical phantom. This timeline is the lifeline of your phantom. To do this, imagine a clock or a calendar right beside your magical phantom. This will communicate to your magical phantom that you are now talking about the element of time, and this element is present in the physical world. Now, tell your magical phantom the limit of its existence. For example, say, "Your lifetime is until ________," or "You shall exist until ___________." You are free to use any other statements that would reflect the same meaning. The important thing here is to communicate to your magical phantom its lifetime limitation.

Giving a time limitation to your magical phantom would be very helpful especially in avoiding any attacks or risks from your magical phantom. This way, even if you lose control of your phantom, it will soon disappear and prevent any undesirable repercussions. Do not worry, if ever you change your mind and want to extend the lifetime of your magical phantom, you can easily do it by recalling your magical phantom. Once your magical phantom is right in front of you, you can reprogram its timeline by following the same procedure as when you first set it up but this time only programming a different timeline for its demise.

It is not absolutely necessary to give a specific timeline to your magical phantom at the very moment of creation. In fact, you may skip this step completely. If you do not set a particular time limit to your magical phantom's existence, just be sure to feed it with energy every now and then to prevent it from disappearing.

The next step is to spend some time imagining your magical phantom already performing its task successfully. This part will further impress upon your magical phantom the task that it has to complete.

The next and final step is to send out your magical phantom into the universe to finally perform its duty. Again, just like the other method that we have already discussed, this can be done with a simple gesture or in any other form that will communicate to your magical phantom that you are finally sending it out into the universe for it to actually act and complete the task that you have given to it.

Once your magical phantom is out and about in the universe, be sure to feed it with magical energy every now and then and take good care of it.

Magical Phantom Upgrade

If you keep your magical phantom for a longer period, it will naturally and on its own upgrade itself. In the beginning, magical phantoms always have very little intelligence and capability. In fact, upon each creation, the only thing that it knows how to do would be the task that you have given to it. That is all that it cares about because that is all that it knows. However, as your magical phantom gains more experience, it will also learn to develop its own skills and abilities.

Now, this natural upgrade in the features of your magical phantom can be either good or bad. It is good in the sense that your magical phantom will become stronger and maybe capable of doing other things for you. However, in the negative sense, this can be a problem if you do not have control over your phantom. This is also why in the previous chapter we have emphasized exercising absolute dominion and control over your magical phantom. The reason for this is that a magical phantom that goes out of the control of a magical practitioner can cause real chaos in the astral plane. And, since the astral plane is connected to the physical realm, then your astral creation, which is your magical phantom, can create actual and real changes in the physical world. Unfortunately, when it reaches this stage, it would be hard to tell if the said change would be something that is desirable for you or not. Once again, it should be emphasized that you must always exercise absolute dominion and control over your magical phantom at all times. Never appear weak before your phantom. Know that to your magical phantom, you are its god; therefore, be sure to act as one. When you are confronting your magical phantom, always act as if you know everything that you are doing and that you are in total control of all things.

Another way to upgrade your magical phantom is through the act of the magus himself. The way to do this is to give another task to your magical phantom. However, take note that you should only do this if your magical phantom has already been in existence for at least a week. This is to make sure that it has already developed some of its magical and psychic faculties and that it would be ready to take on new work. So, how do you go about doing this?

Recall your magical phantom and have it appear right in front of you. Now, you are going to reprogram your magical phantom. This is easy to do, and it is just like us when you first created it. Imagine your magical phantom already performing the new task that you want to give to it. At the same time, give it a verbal command to do the said task. Once again, be sure to formulate your statement in the present tense and abide by the other rules in making a magical affirmation. As you can see, this is just as simple as commanding any other magical phantom, except that you are not commanding a new one but a magical phantom that has already been in existence.

It is up to you if you will make your magical phantom do two things at once, whether you will allow it to continue doing the first task and add the second task or if you will shift its purpose from the first task to the second task alone. In any case, make sure that this is clear to your magical phantom. Still, it is strongly advised that you must only give a single task to your magical phantom at any one time. This way, you can be sure that all its energy will be devoted to a particular point and focus. It is not good to divide the power of your magical phantom into two or more objectives. If you do this, chances are that your magical phantom will not be able to perform with its full force in accomplishing a task. Therefore, the way of the true magus is to only give a single command to the magical phantom at any one time. This will ensure that the whole energy and force of the magical phantom will be fully concentrated into accomplishing the task given to it, thereby significantly increasing its success rate.

The longer that you spend time with your magical phantom, the more that you will get to know it better. With the help of your intuition, you will naturally know just how to deal with your magical phantom especially once it starts acquiring new skills and abilities. However, in case of an emergency and there is a need to obliterate the existence of your magical phantom in order to avoid danger, then you must learn how to kill or destroy your magical creation — and this leads us to our next subject.

How to Obliterate Your Magical Phantom

Obliterating your magical phantom means killing it or simply ending its existence. It should be noted that you must only resort to this technique in extreme cases in order to avoid or stop even in danger. It must be clarified that although you exercise total control and dominion over your magical phantom, you must not abuse your power and become heartless. However, there may come a time when obliterating your magical phantom would be a necessity and will serve the greater good. In this case, then you must gather the courage and exercise that responsibility to put the matter into your own hands and end the life of your magical phantom that has gotten out of control. Having said that, the steps are as follows:

If ever you reach this kind of situation, you can expect that your magical phantom is no longer obeying you as easily as it is supposed to. It may or may not respond when you call it by its name. A simple sign that your magical phantom is getting out of control is when it does not appear to you once you summon it by its name. If you call it by its name and it becomes difficult for it to be summoned, then you should be cautious. So how do you summon your magical phantom if it refuses to return to you even when you call it by its name?

This time, you are going to use some force. To do this, continue to call your magical phantom by its name. The reason behind this is simply to connect your energy to the energy of your magical phantom, and not necessarily to successfully call it. After all, if it refuses to be someone through its name, then really calling it by its name would not be enough. Still, having the name of your magical phantom is something that you could work to your advantage. By using its name, you can easily connect to its energy. Once this connection is established, you can, by force of mind and will, summon your magical phantom back to you and in front of you. To do this, continue to call your magical phantom by its name. But at the same time, also will your magical phantom appear right in front of you by imagining it already right in front of you. It is worth emphasizing that you are the source and creator of your phantom. As such, in accordance with the universal law, no matter how bad or out of control your phantom may have become, it will always be connected to you and subject to your strong will.

Once your magical phantom is right in front of you, imagine a ray of light from the Sun descending to your phantom. Next, see and feel fire burning your magical phantom into nothingness. At this point, you must not show any mercy for your magical phantom. Now is only the time for destruction. Do not worry, you are not completely destroying your magical phantom. You are only transforming it by sending its energy back to the universe where it actually came from.

Only use the said technique in cases of extreme emergency and danger. Nevertheless, when the situation calls that you exercise this power of destruction, be sure to do it without hesitation and with a very strong will.

Questions and Answers

● *How do I know if I have successfully created a magical phantom?*

Beginners normally have so many doubts, especially when they do not trust their magical abilities yet. The key is to practice regularly. Always remember that magic is an art; and, just like any other art form, practice is very important because practice makes perfect. You will know just how successful you are in creating your magical phantom based on the result. If your magical phantom accomplishes the task which, under normal circumstances, could not take place, then you will have more confidence in yourself and in your magical phantom. Continuous experimentation and observation would be very helpful.

- *How can I more effectively manipulate magical energy?*

Other than continuous practice in the art of energy manipulation as we have already discussed, you must be as relaxed as possible. Always remember that it will be easier to harness magical energy the more relaxed you are. The practice of magic is an effort of the mind, not of the physical body. Never forget that all magic is of the mind. You should also meditate regularly. Again, the general rule is to meditate at least twice daily. Continuous practice of meditation will naturally develop your psychic and spiritual faculties. It is also suggested that you meditate for several minutes before you start creating a magical phantom. This way, you will be in the right frame of mind once you actually engage in the practice of magic. When it comes to manipulating magical energy, you should use as many psychic senses as you can. Among all the psychic senses, there are two senses that are very important, and they are the sense of psychic sight and the sense of psychic feeling. By combining these two psychic senses, great and wonderful things can be accomplished by the magus. You should also allow the energy to flow freely. This can easily be done by applying your intention to the flow of energy. Remember the universal principle that energy follows thought. Once the flow of energy is already set in motion, you just allow it to flow without interference. This way, energy can flow like the waters of a river. Master this harmonious flow and manipulation of energy, and you can achieve magical wonders.

- *How many magical phantoms can I create?*

There are no strict rules on the number of magical phantoms that a magician can have under their control and authority. However, if you are a beginner, it is good to manage only one or two magical phantoms at any one time. In the beginning, your objective is to familiarize yourself with the entire process, as well as to gain more experience and confidence. Once you gain more experience and confidence, you can naturally do more. Personally, I know some magical practitioners who only keep one magical phantom. Normally, when you only keep a single magical phantom in your magical journey, it usually creates a very strong bond between the magical practitioner and the phantom. If you find yourself in this situation, just remember never to allow your magical phantom to exceed its function. It is not uncommon to find magical practitioners to develop a strong bond and even mercy for their magical phantom. Just make sure that you are always in full control over your phantom to avoid any future problems and complications. There are also magical practitioners who have a host of magical phantoms under their control all at the same time. If you are this kind of magician, just be sure to take good note of every magical phantom that you are controlling. It is good to write them down on a sheet of paper or a notebook, but just make sure to keep it hidden and that no other person will be able to see it. This way, you can organize and have better supervision over each magical creation that you have. Always remember that you are ultimately and solely responsible for the actions and effects of your magical phantoms.

- *What kind of task can I give to my magical phantom?*

Due to the limited intelligence of a magical phantom, you can literally assign any task to it, and it will do it without discrimination or preference. This is also what makes a magical phantom a very practical and helpful ally. You can use your magical phantom as a form of protective magic, healing magic, motivating magic, and even for sending out communications or messages to others. As you can see, there are no limitations at all except only the limitations that you have placed in your mind. This is also why we practice meditation, so that we can break free from the boundaries that we have unintentionally created in the mind. A magical phantom may also be employed for the benefit of another person. For example, you may send out a magical phantom for the purpose of protecting another person. Indeed, the possibilities are limitless when you work with a magical phantom. However, it must be emphasized as well that you are responsible for all the actions and consequences of your magical phantom. Keep in mind that as its creator, your personal energy is always connected to it. As a basic rule in magic, we must only use our magical powers for good. Another reason for this is that using our magic for evil would mean that we have to face the consequences of the same evil. This is in accordance with the law of karma, which is one of the governing laws of the universe. Whatever we do shall come back to us in one form or another. Never forget this ancient teaching.

● *Can I make my magical phantom physically visible?*

As a general rule, this is not possible simply because a magical phantom exists in the astral dimension, not in the physical realm. However, there may be an exception, and that is when the magical phantom is able to summon and absorb a high level of concentrated energy. In fact, there is a legend of a witch who was able to completely materialize her magical phantom to the point that even laypeople could perceive the phantom. In other words, the magical phantom has taken a physical body. However, I must admit that I still have not met any person who has succeeded in doing the same magical feat. Still, it is doable for your magical phantom to have a direct physical manifestation. A good example of this is when you look at the space where your magical phantom is located and thereby see a hazy or blurry spot. This is usually due to the energy that is in that location, which also happens to be the energy of your magical phantom. I have personally experienced this a few times. Nevertheless, do not be misdirected. Never forget that a magical phantom does not need any physical body for it to be real. After all, magical phantoms belong to the astral dimension, never to the physical plane. In the end, the important thing is that your magical phantom is successfully doing the task that you have given to it.

- *My magical phantom has become aggressive, what can I do?*

When a magical phantom has become aggressive to the point that it is no longer following you, you may try to talk to it and see if it would obey. Exercise your authority as its creator. However, if it still does not cooperate and follow you, then you may have to resort to intentionally and deliberately obliterating it in order to avoid any other complications and dangers. Do not worry, it is quite rare for a magical phantom to become aggressive. In fact, more than 90% of the time, you will find that magical phantoms are very kind and gentle, especially to you who is its creator. Personally, I have created countless magical phantoms and have only encountered about two or three phantoms that turned out aggressive. Still, it is important that you know what you must do in case you find yourself in such a difficult situation.

> ● *I would like to focus more on my magical practices, but I am always too busy with my life. What should I do?*

If you truly want to have any form of real progress in your magical and spiritual life, you must make time for it. You must realize that nobody will prioritize your magical practices but only yourself. In this modern world, it is also very easy to be misdirected and even be manipulated by the world. In fact, the modern world is designed to manipulate people and make them forget who they really are. As a magical practitioner, you must not allow the modern world to control you. The best way of magical practice is to turn the practices into a way of life. If you are really busy with having so many things to do, it may help to have a journal. This way, you will be able to view your life from a different perspective. Find every opportunity that you can to meditate and do all your magical practices. When I was young, I would dedicate late night evenings for my magical practices alone. Of course, this may vary from person to person. The important thing is to take the effort and to actually make time for your real priorities in life. It is also worth noting that having a plan is one thing and actually acting on it is another. If you really want to have any real progress, then you must take positive actions by actually doing what you ought to do as a magical practitioner, and you must do it repeatedly — because this is the way of the true magus.

 • *I still have doubts, what should I do?*

Doubts usually exist in the mind of a beginner. Having doubts is not necessarily bad. In fact, it is good in the sense that it confirms that you are focusing on your practices. However, you must never allow your doubts to limit and control you. The best way to conquer doubts is by engaging in repeated and continuous practice, so that you can experience good results. The more experience you gain, the more confidence you will have, and this will lead to having less doubts. After some time, especially once you have repeated personal experiences pertaining to the magical life, all your doubts will disappear.

 • *Can I make my magical phantom as big as my house?*

There are no rules on the actual appearance of your magical phantom. You are free to make it as small and as big as you want. However, creating a magical phantom that is as big as your house or even as big as the whole earth may have some disadvantages. You must understand that a magical phantom will be much stronger if the energy it possesses is well concentrated. In this regard, it would be beneficial to have a small magical phantom because it is easier to concentrate energy in a small space. Nevertheless, you are still free to create a magical phantom that is as big as your house or even as big as New York. It is not actually the appearance of your magical phantom that matters but its existence and essence in your mind. In fact, you are always free to change the appearance of your magical phantom at any moment. All that you have to do is to imagine your magical phantom right in front of you, and then see and feel it changing into the appearance that you want. In the world of magic and witchcraft, appearances alone do not hold that much weight. It is more important to focus on the essence of energy and its quality than what you can see, for what you can see can change it anytime instantly. It is understandable that in the physical plane the sense of sight plays a very important role. However, in the spiritual and magical planes, the sense of feeling is much more important. This is because appearances in the magical plane can be changed very easily and even instantly. It is not that appearances are not important, but it is just that you could not completely rely on mere appearance alone. You have to see more with your heart than with your eyes.

● *How do I know if magic is really for me?*

This is something that only you yourself can answer. However, it is also something that you cannot simply answer right away immediately. The best and only way to find out is by actually giving it a try. This means that you can pursue the magical path and see how things go for you. It does not matter what reason you may have and why you will pursue this path, but the important thing is to give it a try and see just how it works. Do not worry, you can always turn around and walk away at any time you want. Another important thing to take note of is your own personal happiness. The key here is that the actual path itself should make you happy. If you are pursuing this path only for the goal and objective of gaining supernatural powers, then this path may not be for you. Never forget that the practice of magic is, first and foremost, a spiritual path. Gaining magical power is only a part of the process of soul evolution. If the practices make you happy, then you are most likely called to have this way of life. However, if the practices bore you or if they do not ignite the fire of passion within you, then you may have to look somewhere else for your happiness. Still, the only way to find out is for you to give it an actual try. In any case, you will learn something about yourself which can help you in your life's journey.

A Message

I hope that you have enjoyed reading this book. Having a magical phantom is like having a wonderful ally by your side in your magical journey. It is also worth noting that the practice of creating a magical phantom will also develop your overall psychic and magical faculties, thereby making you a more powerful and effective magical practitioner. As you can see, there is so much that you can learn from this practice, and there is so much that you can gain. Just give it a try and see how it works for you.

If you feel like you could not create a genuine magical phantom after several attempts, do not be discouraged. Just like any other magical craft that is worth learning, it takes practice to master the art of creating a magical phantom. Nevertheless, it is something that is very much worth learning and doing. Do not feel bad. Instead, enjoy every step of the journey and always do your best.

It is also worth remembering that the practice of magic is an art. As an art form, you are free to make adjustments to the techniques that you have learned from this book. In fact, you are strongly encouraged to come up with your own experiments and discoveries. Just like any other books, this book is only just a key that will open the door that will lead you to diverse magical paths. Books can only show you the way, but it is always up to you to take the steps.

If you master the magical art as explained in this book, you will be able to harness and wield so much power. Be sure to use this power only for good. I personally know some magical practitioners who have been blinded by power that they have fallen astray into the wrong path. You must never be like them. You must always stay close to the light, to what is good, and be one with it. The dark arts of magic may be strong, but it will also feel your heart with negativity. Never forget that nothing can overcome the power of love. Even the powers of darkness have no power over it.

It can also be helpful to have a friend or even a group of friends to practice with. However, just make sure to work only with those people who also share the same passion in the magical arts. Be sure to work only with those who are serious and dedicated to the practice of magic. This may not work for everyone, depending on your personal circumstances and personality. Still, it can be beneficial especially if you find someone who also has lots of knowledge pertaining to this magical art. You may also share your knowledge and wisdom with each other.

Always do your best and do not be disappointed if you ever encounter some mistakes and failures along the way. Whenever you can meet a mistake or experience any kind of failure, use it as a way to make yourself stronger. It should also be noted that beginners are very prone to committing many mistakes, and this is actually a good thing because it means that they can learn so much. Remember that every mistake is simply a lesson in disguise. It is just a matter of how you deal with it. By learning from your mistakes and making adjustments to your practices, you will become a more powerful and effective magical practitioner. After some time, you will be surprised as to how much you have grown and matured. The key is to never give up, and that we must simply push forward and continue learning and experiencing the magic of life.

Last but not least, simply enjoy the journey. After all, the practice of magic does not have an end. The path is eternal and infinite, just as the possibilities are also eternal and infinite at every moment. Therefore, always continue to learn, enjoy, always have peace of mind, and be happy. And, whenever you feel that you are not good enough or that you do not belong to this magical universe, just remember this ancient wisdom: You are magic.

Don't miss out!

Visit the website below and you can sign up to receive emails whenever Gideon Crusader publishes a new book. There's no charge and no obligation.

https://books2read.com/r/B-A-VRRV-CHPCC

BOOKS 2 READ

Connecting independent readers to independent writers.

Also by Gideon Crusader

Magic Quest
A Codex on Creating a Magical Phantom